This book belongs to:

A

Name	Date	Time	Service	Price
Address				
Email				
Phone				
Birthday				
Special Requirements				
Notes				

Name	Date	Time	Service	Price
Address				
Email				
Phone				
Birthday				
Special Requirements				
Notes				

Appointments

	Appointments			
Name	**Date**	**Time**	**Service**	**Price**
Address				
Email				
Phone				
Birthday				
Special Requirements				
Notes				

Name	**Date**	**Time**	**Service**	**Price**
Address				
Email				
Phone				
Birthday				
Special Requirements				
Notes				

A

	Appointments			
Name	**Date**	**Time**	**Service**	**Price**
Address				
Email				
Phone				
Birthday				
Special Requirements				
Notes				

	Date	Time	Service	Price
Name	**Date**	**Time**	**Service**	**Price**
Address				
Email				
Phone				
Birthday				
Special Requirements				
Notes				

	Appointments			
Name	Date	Time	Service	Price
Address				
Email				
Phone				
Birthday				
Special Requirements				
Notes				
Name	Date	Time	Service	Price
Address				
Email				
Phone				
Birthday				
Special Requirements				
Notes				

A

Name	Appointments			
	Date	Time	Service	Price
Address				
Email				
Phone				
Birthday				
Special Requirements				
Notes				

Name	Date	Time	Service	Price
Address				
Email				
Phone				
Birthday				
Special Requirements				
Notes				

Name	Date	Time	Service	Price
Appointments				

Name	Date	Time	Service	Price
Address				
Email				
Phone				
Birthday				
Special Requirements				
Notes				

Name	Date	Time	Service	Price
Address				
Email				
Phone				
Birthday				
Special Requirements				
Notes				

B

	Appointments			
Name	**Date**	**Time**	**Service**	**Price**
Address				
Email				
Phone				
Birthday				
Special Requirements				
Notes				
Name	**Date**	**Time**	**Service**	**Price**
Address				
Email				
Phone				
Birthday				
Special Requirements				
Notes				

Name	Date	Time	Service	Price
		Appointments		
Address				
Email				
Phone				
Birthday				
Special Requirements				
Notes				

Name	Date	Time	Service	Price
Address				
Email				
Phone				
Birthday				
Special Requirements				
Notes				

B

	Appointments			
Name	**Date**	**Time**	**Service**	**Price**
Address				
Email				
Phone				
Birthday				
Special Requirements				
Notes				

Name	**Date**	**Time**	**Service**	**Price**
Address				
Email				
Phone				
Birthday				
Special Requirements				
Notes				

Name	Appointments			
	Date	Time	Service	Price
Address				
Email				
Phone				
Birthday				
Special Requirements				
Notes				

Name	Date	Time	Service	Price
Address				
Email				
Phone				
Birthday				
Special Requirements				
Notes				

B

	Appointments			
Name	**Date**	**Time**	**Service**	**Price**
Address				
Email				
Phone				
Birthday				
Special Requirements				
Notes				

Name	**Date**	**Time**	**Service**	**Price**
Address				
Email				
Phone				
Birthday				
Special Requirements				
Notes				

B

Name	Appointments			
	Date	Time	Service	Price
Address				
Email				
Phone				
Birthday				
Special Requirements				
Notes				

Name	Date	Time	Service	Price
Address				
Email				
Phone				
Birthday				
Special Requirements				
Notes				

C

	Appointments			
Name	**Date**	**Time**	**Service**	**Price**
Address				
Email				
Phone				
Birthday				
Special Requirements				
Notes				
Name	**Date**	**Time**	**Service**	**Price**
Address				
Email				
Phone				
Birthday				
Special Requirements				
Notes				

C

Name	Date	Time	Service	Price
Address				
Email				
Phone				
Birthday				
Special Requirements				
Notes				

Name	Date	Time	Service	Price
Address				
Email				
Phone				
Birthday				
Special Requirements				
Notes				

Appointments

C

	Appointments			
Name	**Date**	**Time**	**Service**	**Price**
Address				
Email				
Phone				
Birthday				
Special Requirements				
Notes				

Name	**Date**	**Time**	**Service**	**Price**
Address				
Email				
Phone				
Birthday				
Special Requirements				
Notes				

C

Name	Appointments			
	Date	Time	Service	Price
Address				
Email				
Phone				
Birthday				
Special Requirements				
Notes				

Name	Date	Time	Service	Price
Address				
Email				
Phone				
Birthday				
Special Requirements				
Notes				

C

	Appointments			
Name	**Date**	**Time**	**Service**	**Price**
Address				
Email				
Phone				
Birthday				
Special Requirements				
Notes				

Name	**Date**	**Time**	**Service**	**Price**
Address				
Email				
Phone				
Birthday				
Special Requirements				
Notes				

Name	Appointments			
	Date	Time	Service	Price
Address				
Email				
Phone				
Birthday				
Special Requirements				
Notes				

Name	Date	Time	Service	Price
Address				
Email				
Phone				
Birthday				
Special Requirements				
Notes				

D

	Appointments			
Name	**Date**	**Time**	**Service**	**Price**
Address				
Email				
Phone				
Birthday				
Special Requirements				
Notes				

Name	**Date**	**Time**	**Service**	**Price**
Address				
Email				
Phone				
Birthday				
Special Requirements				
Notes				

Name	Appointments			
	Date	Time	Service	Price
Address				
Email				
Phone				
Birthday				
Special Requirements				
Notes				

Name	Date	Time	Service	Price
Address				
Email				
Phone				
Birthday				
Special Requirements				
Notes				

D

	Appointments			
Name	**Date**	**Time**	**Service**	**Price**
Address				
Email				
Phone				
Birthday				
Special Requirements				
Notes				
Name	**Date**	**Time**	**Service**	**Price**
Address				
Email				
Phone				
Birthday				
Special Requirements				
Notes				

Name	Appointments			
	Date	Time	Service	Price
Address				
Email				
Phone				
Birthday				
Special Requirements				
Notes				

Name	Date	Time	Service	Price
Address				
Email				
Phone				
Birthday				
Special Requirements				
Notes				

D

	Appointments			
Name	**Date**	**Time**	**Service**	**Price**
Address				
Email				
Phone				
Birthday				
Special Requirements				
Notes				

Name	**Date**	**Time**	**Service**	**Price**
Address				
Email				
Phone				
Birthday				
Special Requirements				
Notes				

	Appointments			
Name	**Date**	**Time**	**Service**	**Price**
Address				
Email				
Phone				
Birthday				
Special Requirements				
Notes				

Name	**Date**	**Time**	**Service**	**Price**
Address				
Email				
Phone				
Birthday				
Special Requirements				
Notes				

E

	Appointments			
Name	**Date**	**Time**	**Service**	**Price**
Address				
Email				
Phone				
Birthday				
Special Requirements				
Notes				

Name	**Date**	**Time**	**Service**	**Price**
Address				
Email				
Phone				
Birthday				
Special Requirements				
Notes				

E

Name	Date	Time	Service	Price
Address				
Email				
Phone				
Birthday				
Special Requirements				
Notes				

Name	Date	Time	Service	Price
Address				
Email				
Phone				
Birthday				
Special Requirements				
Notes				

Appointments

E

	Appointments			
Name	**Date**	**Time**	**Service**	**Price**
Address				
Email				
Phone				
Birthday				
Special Requirements				
Notes				
Name	**Date**	**Time**	**Service**	**Price**
Address				
Email				
Phone				
Birthday				
Special Requirements				
Notes				

Name	Appointments			
	Date	Time	Service	Price
Address				
Email				
Phone				
Birthday				
Special Requirements				
Notes				

Name	Date	Time	Service	Price
Address				
Email				
Phone				
Birthday				
Special Requirements				
Notes				

E

	Appointments			
Name	Date	Time	Service	Price
Address				
Email				
Phone				
Birthday				
Special Requirements				
Notes				

Name	Date	Time	Service	Price
Address				
Email				
Phone				
Birthday				
Special Requirements				
Notes				

Name	Appointments			
	Date	Time	Service	Price
Address				
Email				
Phone				
Birthday				
Special Requirements				
Notes				

Name	Date	Time	Service	Price
Address				
Email				
Phone				
Birthday				
Special Requirements				
Notes				

F

	Appointments			
Name	Date	Time	Service	Price
Address				
Email				
Phone				
Birthday				
Special Requirements				
Notes				

Name	Date	Time	Service	Price
Address				
Email				
Phone				
Birthday				
Special Requirements				
Notes				

F

Name	Appointments			
	Date	Time	Service	Price
Address				
Email				
Phone				
Birthday				
Special Requirements				
Notes				

Name	Date	Time	Service	Price
Address				
Email				
Phone				
Birthday				
Special Requirements				
Notes				

F

	Appointments			
Name	**Date**	**Time**	**Service**	**Price**
Address				
Email				
Phone				
Birthday				
Special Requirements				
Notes				

Name	**Date**	**Time**	**Service**	**Price**
Address				
Email				
Phone				
Birthday				
Special Requirements				
Notes				

Name	Date	Time	Service	Price
			Appointments	

Name	Date	Time	Service	Price
Address				
Email				
Phone				
Birthday				
Special Requirements				
Notes				

Name	Date	Time	Service	Price
Address				
Email				
Phone				
Birthday				
Special Requirements				
Notes				

F

	Appointments			
Name	**Date**	**Time**	**Service**	**Price**
Address				
Email				
Phone				
Birthday				
Special Requirements				
Notes				

Name	**Date**	**Time**	**Service**	**Price**
Address				
Email				
Phone				
Birthday				
Special Requirements				
Notes				

Name	Appointments			
	Date	Time	Service	Price
Address				
Email				
Phone				
Birthday				
Special Requirements				
Notes				

Name	Date	Time	Service	Price
Address				
Email				
Phone				
Birthday				
Special Requirements				
Notes				

G

	Appointments			
Name	**Date**	**Time**	**Service**	**Price**
Address				
Email				
Phone				
Birthday				
Special Requirements				
Notes				

Name	**Date**	**Time**	**Service**	**Price**
Address				
Email				
Phone				
Birthday				
Special Requirements				
Notes				

	Appointments			
Name	**Date**	**Time**	**Service**	**Price**
Address				
Email				
Phone				
Birthday				
Special Requirements				
Notes				

Name	**Date**	**Time**	**Service**	**Price**
Address				
Email				
Phone				
Birthday				
Special Requirements				
Notes				

G

	Appointments			
Name	**Date**	**Time**	**Service**	**Price**
Address				
Email				
Phone				
Birthday				
Special Requirements				
Notes				

Name	**Date**	**Time**	**Service**	**Price**
Address				
Email				
Phone				
Birthday				
Special Requirements				
Notes				

Name	Appointments			
	Date	Time	Service	Price
Address				
Email				
Phone				
Birthday				
Special Requirements				
Notes				

Name	Date	Time	Service	Price
Address				
Email				
Phone				
Birthday				
Special Requirements				
Notes				

G

	Appointments			
Name	**Date**	**Time**	**Service**	**Price**
Address				
Email				
Phone				
Birthday				
Special Requirements				
Notes				
Name	**Date**	**Time**	**Service**	**Price**
Address				
Email				
Phone				
Birthday				
Special Requirements				
Notes				

	Appointments			
Name	**Date**	**Time**	**Service**	**Price**
Address				
Email				
Phone				
Birthday				
Special Requirements				
Notes				

Name	**Date**	**Time**	**Service**	**Price**
Address				
Email				
Phone				
Birthday				
Special Requirements				
Notes				

H

	Appointments			
Name	**Date**	**Time**	**Service**	**Price**
Address				
Email				
Phone				
Birthday				
Special Requirements				
Notes				

Name	**Date**	**Time**	**Service**	**Price**
Address				
Email				
Phone				
Birthday				
Special Requirements				
Notes				

Name	Appointments			
	Date	Time	Service	Price
Address				
Email				
Phone				
Birthday				
Special Requirements				
Notes				

Name	Date	Time	Service	Price
Address				
Email				
Phone				
Birthday				
Special Requirements				
Notes				

H

	Appointments			
Name	**Date**	**Time**	**Service**	**Price**
Address				
Email				
Phone				
Birthday				
Special Requirements				
Notes				

Name	**Date**	**Time**	**Service**	**Price**
Address				
Email				
Phone				
Birthday				
Special Requirements				
Notes				

Name	Appointments			
	Date	Time	Service	Price
Address				
Email				
Phone				
Birthday				
Special Requirements				
Notes				

Name	Date	Time	Service	Price
Address				
Email				
Phone				
Birthday				
Special Requirements				
Notes				

H

	Appointments			
Name	**Date**	**Time**	**Service**	**Price**
Address				
Email				
Phone				
Birthday				
Special Requirements				
Notes				

Name	**Date**	**Time**	**Service**	**Price**
Address				
Email				
Phone				
Birthday				
Special Requirements				
Notes				

Name	Appointments			
	Date	Time	Service	Price
Address				
Email				
Phone				
Birthday				
Special Requirements				
Notes				

Name	Date	Time	Service	Price
Address				
Email				
Phone				
Birthday				
Special Requirements				
Notes				

	Appointments			
Name	Date	Time	Service	Price
Address				
Email				
Phone				
Birthday				
Special Requirements				
Notes				

Name	Date	Time	Service	Price
Address				
Email				
Phone				
Birthday				
Special Requirements				
Notes				

	Appointments			
Name	**Date**	**Time**	**Service**	**Price**
Address				
Email				
Phone				
Birthday				
Special Requirements				
Notes				

Name	**Date**	**Time**	**Service**	**Price**
Address				
Email				
Phone				
Birthday				
Special Requirements				
Notes				

	Appointments			
Name	Date	Time	Service	Price
Address				
Email				
Phone				
Birthday				
Special Requirements				
Notes				

Name	Date	Time	Service	Price
Address				
Email				
Phone				
Birthday				
Special Requirements				
Notes				

	Appointments			
Name	**Date**	**Time**	**Service**	**Price**
Address				
Email				
Phone				
Birthday				
Special Requirements				
Notes				

Name	**Date**	**Time**	**Service**	**Price**
Address				
Email				
Phone				
Birthday				
Special Requirements				
Notes				

	Appointments			
Name	**Date**	**Time**	**Service**	**Price**
Address				
Email				
Phone				
Birthday				
Special Requirements				
Notes				

Name	**Date**	**Time**	**Service**	**Price**
Address				
Email				
Phone				
Birthday				
Special Requirements				
Notes				

Name	Appointments			
	Date	Time	Service	Price
Address				
Email				
Phone				
Birthday				
Special Requirements				
Notes				

Name	Date	Time	Service	Price
Address				
Email				
Phone				
Birthday				
Special Requirements				
Notes				

J

Name	Appointments			
	Date	Time	Service	Price
Address				
Email				
Phone				
Birthday				
Special Requirements				
Notes				

Name	Date	Time	Service	Price
Address				
Email				
Phone				
Birthday				
Special Requirements				
Notes				

J

	Appointments			
Name	Date	Time	Service	Price
Address				
Email				
Phone				
Birthday				
Special Requirements				
Notes				

Name	Date	Time	Service	Price
Address				
Email				
Phone				
Birthday				
Special Requirements				
Notes				

J

	Appointments			
Name	**Date**	**Time**	**Service**	**Price**
Address				
Email				
Phone				
Birthday				
Special Requirements				
Notes				

Name	**Date**	**Time**	**Service**	**Price**
Address				
Email				
Phone				
Birthday				
Special Requirements				
Notes				

Name	Appointments			
	Date	Time	Service	Price
Address				
Email				
Phone				
Birthday				
Special Requirements				
Notes				

Name	Date	Time	Service	Price
Address				
Email				
Phone				
Birthday				
Special Requirements				
Notes				

J

	Appointments			
Name	Date	Time	Service	Price
Address				
Email				
Phone				
Birthday				
Special Requirements				
Notes				
Name	Date	Time	Service	Price
Address				
Email				
Phone				
Birthday				
Special Requirements				
Notes				

Name	Appointments			
	Date	Time	Service	Price
Address				
Email				
Phone				
Birthday				
Special Requirements				
Notes				

Name	Date	Time	Service	Price
Address				
Email				
Phone				
Birthday				
Special Requirements				
Notes				

K

Name	Appointments			
	Date	Time	Service	Price
Address				
Email				
Phone				
Birthday				
Special Requirements				
Notes				

Name	Date	Time	Service	Price
Address				
Email				
Phone				
Birthday				
Special Requirements				
Notes				

K

Name	Appointments			
	Date	Time	Service	Price
Address				
Email				
Phone				
Birthday				
Special Requirements				
Notes				

Name	Date	Time	Service	Price
Address				
Email				
Phone				
Birthday				
Special Requirements				
Notes				

K

	Appointments			
Name	Date	Time	Service	Price
Address				
Email				
Phone				
Birthday				
Special Requirements				
Notes				

Name	Date	Time	Service	Price
Address				
Email				
Phone				
Birthday				
Special Requirements				
Notes				

Name	Appointments			
	Date	Time	Service	Price
Address				
Email				
Phone				
Birthday				
Special Requirements				
Notes				

Name	Date	Time	Service	Price
Address				
Email				
Phone				
Birthday				
Special Requirements				
Notes				

K

Name	Appointments			
	Date	Time	Service	Price
Address				
Email				
Phone				
Birthday				
Special Requirements				
Notes				

Name	Date	Time	Service	Price
Address				
Email				
Phone				
Birthday				
Special Requirements				
Notes				

Name	Date	Time	Service	Price
Appointments				
Name	Date	Time	Service	Price
Address				
Email				
Phone				
Birthday				
Special Requirements				
Notes				

Name	Date	Time	Service	Price
Address				
Email				
Phone				
Birthday				
Special Requirements				
Notes				

L

	Appointments			
Name	**Date**	**Time**	**Service**	**Price**
Address				
Email				
Phone				
Birthday				
Special Requirements				
Notes				

Name	**Date**	**Time**	**Service**	**Price**
Address				
Email				
Phone				
Birthday				
Special Requirements				
Notes				

Name	Date	Time	Service	Price
			Appointments	
Address				
Email				
Phone				
Birthday				
Special Requirements				
Notes				

Name	Date	Time	Service	Price
Address				
Email				
Phone				
Birthday				
Special Requirements				
Notes				

L

	Appointments			
Name	**Date**	**Time**	**Service**	**Price**
Address				
Email				
Phone				
Birthday				
Special Requirements				
Notes				

Name	**Date**	**Time**	**Service**	**Price**
Address				
Email				
Phone				
Birthday				
Special Requirements				
Notes				

L

	Appointments			
Name	**Date**	**Time**	**Service**	**Price**
Address				
Email				
Phone				
Birthday				
Special Requirements				
Notes				

Name	**Date**	**Time**	**Service**	**Price**
Address				
Email				
Phone				
Birthday				
Special Requirements				
Notes				

L

Appointments				
Name	**Date**	**Time**	**Service**	**Price**
Address				
Email				
Phone				
Birthday				
Special Requirements				
Notes				

Name	**Date**	**Time**	**Service**	**Price**
Address				
Email				
Phone				
Birthday				
Special Requirements				
Notes				

L

Name	Date	Time	Service	Price
Address				
Email				
Phone				
Birthday				
Special Requirements				
Notes				

Name	Date	Time	Service	Price
Address				
Email				
Phone				
Birthday				
Special Requirements				
Notes				

Appointments

Name	Appointments			
	Date	Time	Service	Price
Address				
Email				
Phone				
Birthday				
Special Requirements				
Notes				

Name	Date	Time	Service	Price
Address				
Email				
Phone				
Birthday				
Special Requirements				
Notes				

Name	Date	Time	Service	Price
Address				
Email				
Phone				
Birthday				
Special Requirements				
Notes				

Name	Date	Time	Service	Price
Address				
Email				
Phone				
Birthday				
Special Requirements				
Notes				

M

Name	Appointments			
	Date	Time	Service	Price
Address				
Email				
Phone				
Birthday				
Special Requirements				
Notes				

Name	Date	Time	Service	Price
Address				
Email				
Phone				
Birthday				
Special Requirements				
Notes				

M

Name	Appointments			
	Date	Time	Service	Price
Address				
Email				
Phone				
Birthday				
Special Requirements				
Notes				

Name	Date	Time	Service	Price
Address				
Email				
Phone				
Birthday				
Special Requirements				
Notes				

M

Name		Appointments			
	Date	Time	Service	Price
Address					
Email					
Phone					
Birthday					
Special Requirements					
Notes					

Name	Date	Time	Service	Price
Address				
Email				
Phone				
Birthday				
Special Requirements				
Notes				

M

Name	Appointments			
	Date	Time	Service	Price
Address				
Email				
Phone				
Birthday				
Special Requirements				
Notes				

Name	Date	Time	Service	Price
Address				
Email				
Phone				
Birthday				
Special Requirements				
Notes				

N

	Appointments			
Name	Date	Time	Service	Price
Address				
Email				
Phone				
Birthday				
Special Requirements				
Notes				

Name	Date	Time	Service	Price
Address				
Email				
Phone				
Birthday				
Special Requirements				
Notes				

Name	Appointments			
	Date	Time	Service	Price
Address				
Email				
Phone				
Birthday				
Special Requirements				
Notes				

Name	Date	Time	Service	Price
Address				
Email				
Phone				
Birthday				
Special Requirements				
Notes				

N

	Appointments			
Name	**Date**	**Time**	**Service**	**Price**
Address				
Email				
Phone				
Birthday				
Special Requirements				
Notes				

Name	**Date**	**Time**	**Service**	**Price**
Address				
Email				
Phone				
Birthday				
Special Requirements				
Notes				

Name	Date	Time	Service	Price
		Appointments		
Address				
Email				
Phone				
Birthday				
Special Requirements				
Notes				

Name	Date	Time	Service	Price
Address				
Email				
Phone				
Birthday				
Special Requirements				
Notes				

N

Name	Appointments			
	Date	Time	Service	Price
Address				
Email				
Phone				
Birthday				
Special Requirements				
Notes				

Name	Date	Time	Service	Price
Address				
Email				
Phone				
Birthday				
Special Requirements				
Notes				

N

Name	Date	Time	Service	Price
Address				
Email				
Phone				
Birthday				
Special Requirements				
Notes				

Name	Date	Time	Service	Price
Address				
Email				
Phone				
Birthday				
Special Requirements				
Notes				

O

Name	Appointments			
	Date	Time	Service	Price
Address				
Email				
Phone				
Birthday				
Special Requirements				
Notes				

Name	Date	Time	Service	Price
Address				
Email				
Phone				
Birthday				
Special Requirements				
Notes				

O

Name	Date	Time	Service	Price
Address				
Email				
Phone				
Birthday				
Special Requirements				
Notes				

Name	Date	Time	Service	Price
Address				
Email				
Phone				
Birthday				
Special Requirements				
Notes				

Appointments

O

	Appointments			
Name	Date	Time	Service	Price
Address				
Email				
Phone				
Birthday				
Special Requirements				
Notes				

Name	Date	Time	Service	Price
Address				
Email				
Phone				
Birthday				
Special Requirements				
Notes				

O

	Appointments			
Name	Date	Time	Service	Price
Address				
Email				
Phone				
Birthday				
Special Requirements				
Notes				

Name	Date	Time	Service	Price
Address				
Email				
Phone				
Birthday				
Special Requirements				
Notes				

O

Name	Appointments			
	Date	Time	Service	Price
Address				
Email				
Phone				
Birthday				
Special Requirements				
Notes				

Name	Date	Time	Service	Price
Address				
Email				
Phone				
Birthday				
Special Requirements				
Notes				

Name	Date	Time	Service	Price
Appointments				
Address				
Email				
Phone				
Birthday				
Special Requirements				
Notes				

Name	Date	Time	Service	Price
Address				
Email				
Phone				
Birthday				
Special Requirements				
Notes				

P

	Appointments			
Name	**Date**	**Time**	**Service**	**Price**
Address				
Email				
Phone				
Birthday				
Special Requirements				
Notes				

Name	**Date**	**Time**	**Service**	**Price**
Address				
Email				
Phone				
Birthday				
Special Requirements				
Notes				

	Appointments			
Name	**Date**	**Time**	**Service**	**Price**
Address				
Email				
Phone				
Birthday				
Special Requirements				
Notes				

Name	**Date**	**Time**	**Service**	**Price**
Address				
Email				
Phone				
Birthday				
Special Requirements				
Notes				

P

	Appointments			
Name	**Date**	**Time**	**Service**	**Price**
Address				
Email				
Phone				
Birthday				
Special Requirements				
Notes				

Name	**Date**	**Time**	**Service**	**Price**
Address				
Email				
Phone				
Birthday				
Special Requirements				
Notes				

P

Name	Date	Time	Service	Price
Address				
Email				
Phone				
Birthday				
Special Requirements				
Notes				

Name	Date	Time	Service	Price
Address				
Email				
Phone				
Birthday				
Special Requirements				
Notes				

Appointments

P

	Appointments			
Name	**Date**	**Time**	**Service**	**Price**
Address				
Email				
Phone				
Birthday				
Special Requirements				
Notes				

Name	**Date**	**Time**	**Service**	**Price**
Address				
Email				
Phone				
Birthday				
Special Requirements				
Notes				

Name	Appointments			
	Date	Time	Service	Price
Address				
Email				
Phone				
Birthday				
Special Requirements				
Notes				

Name	Date	Time	Service	Price
Address				
Email				
Phone				
Birthday				
Special Requirements				
Notes				

Q

	Appointments			
Name	**Date**	**Time**	**Service**	**Price**
Address				
Email				
Phone				
Birthday				
Special Requirements				
Notes				

Name	**Date**	**Time**	**Service**	**Price**
Address				
Email				
Phone				
Birthday				
Special Requirements				
Notes				

Q

	Appointments			
Name	**Date**	**Time**	**Service**	**Price**
Address				
Email				
Phone				
Birthday				
Special Requirements				
Notes				

Name	**Date**	**Time**	**Service**	**Price**
Address				
Email				
Phone				
Birthday				
Special Requirements				
Notes				

Q

	Appointments			
Name	**Date**	**Time**	**Service**	**Price**
Address				
Email				
Phone				
Birthday				
Special Requirements				
Notes				

Name	**Date**	**Time**	**Service**	**Price**
Address				
Email				
Phone				
Birthday				
Special Requirements				
Notes				

	Appointments			
Name	**Date**	**Time**	**Service**	**Price**
Address				
Email				
Phone				
Birthday				
Special Requirements				
Notes				

Name	**Date**	**Time**	**Service**	**Price**
Address				
Email				
Phone				
Birthday				
Special Requirements				
Notes				

Q

	Appointments			
Name	**Date**	**Time**	**Service**	**Price**
Address				
Email				
Phone				
Birthday				
Special Requirements				
Notes				
Name	**Date**	**Time**	**Service**	**Price**
Address				
Email				
Phone				
Birthday				
Special Requirements				
Notes				

Q

	Appointments			
Name	Date	Time	Service	Price
Address				
Email				
Phone				
Birthday				
Special Requirements				
Notes				
Name	Date	Time	Service	Price
Address				
Email				
Phone				
Birthday				
Special Requirements				
Notes				

R

	Appointments			
Name	**Date**	**Time**	**Service**	**Price**
Address				
Email				
Phone				
Birthday				
Special Requirements				
Notes				

Name	**Date**	**Time**	**Service**	**Price**
Address				
Email				
Phone				
Birthday				
Special Requirements				
Notes				

Name	Appointments			
	Date	Time	Service	Price
Address				
Email				
Phone				
Birthday				
Special Requirements				
Notes				

Name	Date	Time	Service	Price
Address				
Email				
Phone				
Birthday				
Special Requirements				
Notes				

R

	Appointments			
Name	**Date**	**Time**	**Service**	**Price**
Address				
Email				
Phone				
Birthday				
Special Requirements				
Notes				

Name	**Date**	**Time**	**Service**	**Price**
Address				
Email				
Phone				
Birthday				
Special Requirements				
Notes				

Name	Appointments			
	Date	Time	Service	Price
Address				
Email				
Phone				
Birthday				
Special Requirements				
Notes				

Name	Date	Time	Service	Price
Address				
Email				
Phone				
Birthday				
Special Requirements				
Notes				

R

	Appointments			
Name	**Date**	**Time**	**Service**	**Price**
Address				
Email				
Phone				
Birthday				
Special Requirements				
Notes				

Name	**Date**	**Time**	**Service**	**Price**
Address				
Email				
Phone				
Birthday				
Special Requirements				
Notes				

Name	Appointments			
	Date	Time	Service	Price
Address				
Email				
Phone				
Birthday				
Special Requirements				
Notes				

Name	Date	Time	Service	Price
Address				
Email				
Phone				
Birthday				
Special Requirements				
Notes				

S

Appointments				
Name	**Date**	**Time**	**Service**	**Price**
Address				
Email				
Phone				
Birthday				
Special Requirements				
Notes				

Name	**Date**	**Time**	**Service**	**Price**
Address				
Email				
Phone				
Birthday				
Special Requirements				
Notes				

Name	Appointments			
	Date	Time	Service	Price
Address				
Email				
Phone				
Birthday				
Special Requirements				
Notes				

Name	Date	Time	Service	Price
Address				
Email				
Phone				
Birthday				
Special Requirements				
Notes				

S

Name	Appointments			
	Date	Time	Service	Price
Address				
Email				
Phone				
Birthday				
Special Requirements				
Notes				

Name	Date	Time	Service	Price
Address				
Email				
Phone				
Birthday				
Special Requirements				
Notes				

Name	Appointments			
	Date	Time	Service	Price
Address				
Email				
Phone				
Birthday				
Special Requirements				
Notes				

Name	Date	Time	Service	Price
Address				
Email				
Phone				
Birthday				
Special Requirements				
Notes				

S

	Appointments			
Name	Date	Time	Service	Price
Address				
Email				
Phone				
Birthday				
Special Requirements				
Notes				
Name	Date	Time	Service	Price
Address				
Email				
Phone				
Birthday				
Special Requirements				
Notes				

	Appointments			
Name	**Date**	**Time**	**Service**	**Price**
Address				
Email				
Phone				
Birthday				
Special Requirements				
Notes				

Name	**Date**	**Time**	**Service**	**Price**
Address				
Email				
Phone				
Birthday				
Special Requirements				
Notes				

T

	Appointments			
Name	**Date**	**Time**	**Service**	**Price**
Address				
Email				
Phone				
Birthday				
Special Requirements				
Notes				

Name	**Date**	**Time**	**Service**	**Price**
Address				
Email				
Phone				
Birthday				
Special Requirements				
Notes				

T

Name					

	Appointments			
Name	Date	Time	Service	Price
Address				
Email				
Phone				
Birthday				
Special Requirements				
Notes				

Name	Date	Time	Service	Price
Address				
Email				
Phone				
Birthday				
Special Requirements				
Notes				

T

	Appointments			
Name	**Date**	**Time**	**Service**	**Price**
Address				
Email				
Phone				
Birthday				
Special Requirements				
Notes				

Name	**Date**	**Time**	**Service**	**Price**
Address				
Email				
Phone				
Birthday				
Special Requirements				
Notes				

T

Name	Date	Time	Service	Price
Address				
Email				
Phone				
Birthday				
Special Requirements				
Notes				

Name	Date	Time	Service	Price
Address				
Email				
Phone				
Birthday				
Special Requirements				
Notes				

Appointments

T

	Appointments			
Name	Date	Time	Service	Price
Address				
Email				
Phone				
Birthday				
Special Requirements				
Notes				
Name	Date	Time	Service	Price
Address				
Email				
Phone				
Birthday				
Special Requirements				
Notes				

T

Name	Appointments			
	Date	Time	Service	Price
Address				
Email				
Phone				
Birthday				
Special Requirements				
Notes				

Name	Date	Time	Service	Price
Address				
Email				
Phone				
Birthday				
Special Requirements				
Notes				

U

	Appointments			
Name	**Date**	**Time**	**Service**	**Price**
Address				
Email				
Phone				
Birthday				
Special Requirements				
Notes				

Name	**Date**	**Time**	**Service**	**Price**
Address				
Email				
Phone				
Birthday				
Special Requirements				
Notes				

Name	Appointments			
	Date	Time	Service	Price
Address				
Email				
Phone				
Birthday				
Special Requirements				
Notes				

Name	Date	Time	Service	Price
Address				
Email				
Phone				
Birthday				
Special Requirements				
Notes				

U

	Appointments			
Name	**Date**	**Time**	**Service**	**Price**
Address				
Email				
Phone				
Birthday				
Special Requirements				
Notes				

Name	**Date**	**Time**	**Service**	**Price**
Address				
Email				
Phone				
Birthday				
Special Requirements				
Notes				

Name	Appointments			
	Date	Time	Service	Price
Address				
Email				
Phone				
Birthday				
Special Requirements				
Notes				

Name	Date	Time	Service	Price
Address				
Email				
Phone				
Birthday				
Special Requirements				
Notes				

U

	Appointments			
Name	Date	Time	Service	Price
Address				
Email				
Phone				
Birthday				
Special Requirements				
Notes				
Name	Date	Time	Service	Price
Address				
Email				
Phone				
Birthday				
Special Requirements				
Notes				

U

Name		Appointments			
	Date	Time	Service	Price
Address					
Email					
Phone					
Birthday					
Special Requirements					
Notes					

Name	Date	Time	Service	Price
Address				
Email				
Phone				
Birthday				
Special Requirements				
Notes				

V

Appointments				
Name	Date	Time	Service	Price
Address				
Email				
Phone				
Birthday				
Special Requirements				
Notes				

Name	Date	Time	Service	Price
Address				
Email				
Phone				
Birthday				
Special Requirements				
Notes				

V

	Appointments			
Name	**Date**	**Time**	**Service**	**Price**
Address				
Email				
Phone				
Birthday				
Special Requirements				
Notes				

Name	**Date**	**Time**	**Service**	**Price**
Address				
Email				
Phone				
Birthday				
Special Requirements				
Notes				

V

	Appointments			
Name	**Date**	**Time**	**Service**	**Price**
Address				
Email				
Phone				
Birthday				
Special Requirements				
Notes				

Name	**Date**	**Time**	**Service**	**Price**
Address				
Email				
Phone				
Birthday				
Special Requirements				
Notes				

Name	Appointments			
	Date	Time	Service	Price
Address				
Email				
Phone				
Birthday				
Special Requirements				
Notes				

Name	Date	Time	Service	Price
Address				
Email				
Phone				
Birthday				
Special Requirements				
Notes				

V

	Appointments			
Name	Date	Time	Service	Price
Address				
Email				
Phone				
Birthday				
Special Requirements				
Notes				
Name	Date	Time	Service	Price
Address				
Email				
Phone				
Birthday				
Special Requirements				
Notes				

V

	Appointments			
Name	**Date**	**Time**	**Service**	**Price**
Address				
Email				
Phone				
Birthday				
Special Requirements				
Notes				

Name	**Date**	**Time**	**Service**	**Price**
Address				
Email				
Phone				
Birthday				
Special Requirements				
Notes				

Name	Appointments			
	Date	Time	Service	Price
Address				
Email				
Phone				
Birthday				
Special Requirements				
Notes				

Name	Date	Time	Service	Price
Address				
Email				
Phone				
Birthday				
Special Requirements				
Notes				

	Appointments			
Name	**Date**	**Time**	**Service**	**Price**
Address				
Email				
Phone				
Birthday				
Special Requirements				
Notes				

Name	**Date**	**Time**	**Service**	**Price**
Address				
Email				
Phone				
Birthday				
Special Requirements				
Notes				

Name	Appointments			
	Date	Time	Service	Price
Address				
Email				
Phone				
Birthday				
Special Requirements				
Notes				

Name	Date	Time	Service	Price
Address				
Email				
Phone				
Birthday				
Special Requirements				
Notes				

	Appointments			
Name	Date	Time	Service	Price
Address				
Email				
Phone				
Birthday				
Special Requirements				
Notes				
Name	Date	Time	Service	Price
Address				
Email				
Phone				
Birthday				
Special Requirements				
Notes				

W

Name	Appointments			
	Date	Time	Service	Price
Address				
Email				
Phone				
Birthday				
Special Requirements				
Notes				

Name	Date	Time	Service	Price
Address				
Email				
Phone				
Birthday				
Special Requirements				
Notes				

Name	Appointments			
	Date	Time	Service	Price
Address				
Email				
Phone				
Birthday				
Special Requirements				
Notes				

Name	Date	Time	Service	Price
Address				
Email				
Phone				
Birthday				
Special Requirements				
Notes				

X

	Appointments			
Name	**Date**	**Time**	**Service**	**Price**
Address				
Email				
Phone				
Birthday				
Special Requirements				
Notes				

Name	**Date**	**Time**	**Service**	**Price**
Address				
Email				
Phone				
Birthday				
Special Requirements				
Notes				

X

Appointments				
Name	Date	Time	Service	Price
Address				
Email				
Phone				
Birthday				
Special Requirements				
Notes				

Name	Date	Time	Service	Price
Address				
Email				
Phone				
Birthday				
Special Requirements				
Notes				

X

	Appointments			
Name	**Date**	**Time**	**Service**	**Price**
Address				
Email				
Phone				
Birthday				
Special Requirements				
Notes				

Name	**Date**	**Time**	**Service**	**Price**
Address				
Email				
Phone				
Birthday				
Special Requirements				
Notes				

Name	Appointments			
	Date	Time	Service	Price
Address				
Email				
Phone				
Birthday				
Special Requirements				
Notes				

Name	Date	Time	Service	Price
Address				
Email				
Phone				
Birthday				
Special Requirements				
Notes				

X

Name	Appointments			
	Date	Time	Service	Price
Address				
Email				
Phone				
Birthday				
Special Requirements				
Notes				

Name	Date	Time	Service	Price
Address				
Email				
Phone				
Birthday				
Special Requirements				
Notes				

X

Name	Appointments			
	Date	Time	Service	Price
Address				
Email				
Phone				
Birthday				
Special Requirements				
Notes				

Name	Date	Time	Service	Price
Address				
Email				
Phone				
Birthday				
Special Requirements				
Notes				

Y

	Appointments			
Name	**Date**	**Time**	**Service**	**Price**
Address				
Email				
Phone				
Birthday				
Special Requirements				
Notes				

Name	**Date**	**Time**	**Service**	**Price**
Address				
Email				
Phone				
Birthday				
Special Requirements				
Notes				

Name	Appointments			
	Date	Time	Service	Price
Address				
Email				
Phone				
Birthday				
Special Requirements				
Notes				

Name	Date	Time	Service	Price
Address				
Email				
Phone				
Birthday				
Special Requirements				
Notes				

Y

Name	Appointments			
	Date	Time	Service	Price
Address				
Email				
Phone				
Birthday				
Special Requirements				
Notes				

Name	Date	Time	Service	Price
Address				
Email				
Phone				
Birthday				
Special Requirements				
Notes				

Y

| Name | Appointments | | | |
	Date	Time	Service	Price
Address				
Email				
Phone				
Birthday				
Special Requirements				
Notes				

Name	Date	Time	Service	Price
Address				
Email				
Phone				
Birthday				
Special Requirements				
Notes				

Y

Name	Appointments			
	Date	Time	Service	Price
Address				
Email				
Phone				
Birthday				
Special Requirements				
Notes				

Name	Date	Time	Service	Price
Address				
Email				
Phone				
Birthday				
Special Requirements				
Notes				

Name	Appointments			
	Date	Time	Service	Price
Address				
Email				
Phone				
Birthday				
Special Requirements				
Notes				

Name	Date	Time	Service	Price
Address				
Email				
Phone				
Birthday				
Special Requirements				
Notes				

Z

	Appointments			
Name	**Date**	**Time**	**Service**	**Price**
Address				
Email				
Phone				
Birthday				
Special Requirements				
Notes				

Name	**Date**	**Time**	**Service**	**Price**
Address				
Email				
Phone				
Birthday				
Special Requirements				
Notes				

Name	Appointments			
	Date	Time	Service	Price
Address				
Email				
Phone				
Birthday				
Special Requirements				
Notes				

Name	Date	Time	Service	Price
Address				
Email				
Phone				
Birthday				
Special Requirements				
Notes				

Z

	Appointments			
Name	**Date**	**Time**	**Service**	**Price**
Address				
Email				
Phone				
Birthday				
Special Requirements				
Notes				

Name	**Date**	**Time**	**Service**	**Price**
Address				
Email				
Phone				
Birthday				
Special Requirements				
Notes				

Z

Name	Date	Time	Service	Price
Address				
Email				
Phone				
Birthday				
Special Requirements				
Notes				

Appointments

Name	Date	Time	Service	Price
Address				
Email				
Phone				
Birthday				
Special Requirements				
Notes				

Z

Name	Appointments			
	Date	Time	Service	Price
Address				
Email				
Phone				
Birthday				
Special Requirements				
Notes				

Name	Date	Time	Service	Price
Address				
Email				
Phone				
Birthday				
Special Requirements				
Notes				